Low Oxalate Fresh and Fast Cookbook

Melinda Keen

Copyright © 2015 Melinda Keen
All rights reserved.
ISBN: 1511675918
ISBN-13: 978-1511675918

DEDICATION

In dedication to my Lord
for making me who I am
and for His leadership in my life.

※

I'd like to thank my editor
Jessica Matthews
for her time and her professionalism.
With a great eye for detail she caught my careless errors.
Her remarks and suggestions were excellent and I'm so grateful for her outstanding work.

CONTENTS

Introduction	7
Ingredients	8
Free Foods & Tapioca Buns	12
My Story	14
Resources	77
Baked Lemon Rosemary Chicken	16
Chicken Caesar Salad	18
Chicken Gumbo with Effortless Roux	20
Chicken Lentils	22
Fish Fritters with Sweet & Spicy Sauce	24
Garden Pasta	26
Ground Beef Stir-Fry	28
Herbed Salmon on Creamy Pea & Corn Bed	30
Jamaican Jerk Thighs	32
Loaded Beef Burger	34
Lo-Ox Chili	36
Mahi Mahi with Artichoke Hearts	38
Oriental Soup	40
Pizza Casserole	42
Salmon Pasta Casserole	44
Salmon Patties with Easy Cheesy Asparagus	46
Seared Mahi Mahi Salad	48
Slow Cooker Barbecue Chicken	50
Slow Cooker Chicken Garden Pasta	52
Slow Cooker Indian Chicken	54
Slow Cooker Meatloaf Meal	56
Slow Cooker Tamale Pie	58
Slow Cooker Unstuffed Cabbage	60
Steak & Brussels Sprout Hash	62
Superfood Soup	64
Sweet & Spicy Stir-Fry	66
Taco Salad	68
Turkey Sausage Casserole	70
Vegetable Egg Stir-Fry	72
Very Veggie Spaghetti	74

INTRODUCTION

Learn how simple it can be to put delicious, nutritious, home-cooked, low oxalate meals (40 to 50 mg each day) on the table in 30 minutes or less. You'll discover healthy original recipes that include casseroles, pastas, soups, stir-fries, and slow cooker meals with quick and easy prep time. Most recipes yield 2 or 4 ample servings and all of them can be easily doubled.

All recipes include nutrient-dense, additive-free, wholesome foods such as fresh vegetables, grass-fed beef, wild-caught fish, and pasture-raised poultry and eggs. The three healthy fats I use in these recipes are unrefined coconut oil, extra virgin olive oil, and butter made from grass-fed cows. These are the healthy fats readily available to me at a reasonable price. Emerging evidence suggests most people need about 50-70 percent of their diet (calories) as healthy fats. Many vital bodily functions depend on the presence of healthy fats in your diet.

Most of these meals are high in key vitamins and minerals for the low oxalate dieter. Oxalates strongly bind to calcium, magnesium, zinc and potassium and reduces the absorption of these minerals; therefore, it's important to consume these minerals in high amounts via the diet to optimize your health. Vitamins B6, D and K also help the body handle oxalates. In the "Cook's Note" section I've noted recipes high in these vitamins.

I love to cook, because I love to eat. Feeling energetic and healthy is important to me as well. Therefore, even though I work a full time job, I prepare a wholesome, fresh from scratch, highly nutritious, non-toxic meal most nights of the week. Most of my recipes are either on the table in 30 minutes or less or hot and ready in the slow cooker when I arrive home from work. Preparing meals at home allows me to control the ingredients in a meal and feel a sense of wellbeing. I believe the most important and the most powerful tool you have to change your health is knowing what you're putting in your body. Our bodies are equipped with an amazing healing ability if it's provided with the foods it's designed for.

INGREDIENTS

I believe that choosing foods that are as close to their natural state as possible is the key to a long healthy life. Another key part of a healthy diet is the absence of toxic chemicals. We should be eating foods that will nourish the body, like clean, whole, pesticide and hormone free products. This means cutting out processed foods and replacing them with natural whole foods such as dairy, fruits, vegetables, herbs, meats and eggs. Good fats are also beneficial and should constitute half or more of the calories in a healthy diet.

Dairy

Regardless of whether you opt for raw, organic lightly pasteurized, or organic pasteurized, the full-fat version is the healthier choice. When the fat is removed from milk, what remains are a significant number of fat-soluble vitamins that can't be absorbed as well as an overabundance of lactose. I use dairy products in my recipes because the calcium from dairy binds with oxalates from foods, so the body doesn't absorb the oxalate. Dairy contains negligible amounts of oxalate.

Fats

Most of my recipes are made with grass-fed cow's milk butter, organic unrefined coconut oil, and extra-virgin olive oil. Butter, especially from grass-fed cows, is a natural healthy alternative to unnatural and harmful partially hydrogenated vegetable oils, margarines and shortenings or genetically modified oils. Coconut oil is the healthiest fat for frying and sautéing because it can withstand high heat without altering chemically. Unrefined coconut oil has the flavor of fresh coconuts since it is not deodorized or chemically processed. It is rich in proteins, vitamins, and antioxidants. Extra virgin olive oil is a healthy fat to include in your diet if it's not over heated. It would not be the best frying oil to use. If the oil is truly extra virgin it has a distinctive taste and is high in antioxidants. Butter, coconut oil, and olive oil contain negligible amounts of oxalate.

Fruits and Vegetables

It is better to eat fruits and vegetables grown organically, but if budget or availability restricts your choice, remove outer leaves or peels and wash thoroughly. Organic growers are prohibited from using synthetic pesticides that have harmful effects on your health. Buy fresh and ripe fruits and vegetables when they are in season. Otherwise choose frozen. Frozen produce is processed at peak ripeness and is the most nutrient-packed. My recipes rarely include canned vegetables. My concern is their sodium content, as sodium is often added to help maintain the flavor of vegetables during the canning process. When I do use them, and it's usually because I can't find them fresh or frozen, I rinse them well in a colander. At times, I do choose food in jars, such as jams and tomato sauces, simply to save time. Buying an organic product is important for health and nutrition, but just as important for low oxalate dieters is checking the ingredients list for high oxalate food. Fruits and vegetables have a wide range of oxalate contents. The recipes in this cookbook do not contain fruits and vegetables in the high oxalate range.

Herbs & Spices

Beyond adding flavor, herbs and spices carry unique antioxidants, phytosterols, and many other nutrient substances that help our body fight germs and boosts the immune system. Fresh herbs are more readily available during summer months, especially if you grow your own, but some do better when they are dried. Basically, fresh herbs and spices are added near the end of a dish or at the finish, and dried ones are best added during the cooking so the flavor has time to infuse the whole dish. It is best to choose organic herbs and spices due to the fact that these are plants that are conventionally grown with the use of pesticides. Herbs and spices have a wide range of oxalate contents. The recipes in this cookbook do not contain herbs and spices in the high oxalate range.

Pepper comes from the fruit of the pepper plant. The peppercorns are processed two different ways. Black peppercorns are sun-dried to turn the pepper black, and to produce white pepper the outer layer is removed leaving only the inner seed. The high oxalate content of black pepper comes from the outer layer of the peppercorn. Therefore, white pepper is low in oxalate content and preferred in all of my recipes. If you prefer, small amounts of black pepper can be used in these recipes.

Salt
Sea salt and table salt have the same basic nutritional value. I use sea salt or pink Himalayan salt in my recipes because table salt is more heavily processed to eliminate minerals and usually contains an additive to prevent clumping.

Meat, Fish, and Eggs
For optimal health I choose grass-fed organic beef and lamb, pasture raised turkey and chicken, wild-caught fish and pasture-raised organic eggs. In order to be certified to the US Department of Agriculture's (USDA) organic standards farms and ranches must follow a strict set of guidelines. The animals' organic feed cannot contain animal by-products, antibiotics or genetically engineered grains and cannot be grown using pesticides or chemical fertilizers. No antibiotics or added growth hormones are allowed, and they must have outdoor access. If you prefer to replace some of the meats with pork I highly recommend you find a naturally raised, pastured source. Pork can have a lot of contaminants, including the controversial drug ractopamine, which is banned in many parts of the world. Farm-raised fish commonly contains high levels of contaminants as well. Farmed fish are fed an unnatural diet of grains and legumes. The healthiest choice would be wild-caught fish. These fish tend to be higher in Omega 3 fatty acids and contain very low levels of disease as well as being free from antibiotics and pesticides. All meats, fish, and eggs contain negligible amounts of oxalate.

Grains
Most of my recipes do not include grains because most grains are high in oxalates. White rice and plain pasta are relatively low in oxalates, so I add these to my meals occasionally. Corn, cornmeal and corn tortilla chips are sometimes listed as having low, sometimes medium oxalate content; therefore, I limit these foods to rare occasions or when I'm sure there are no other oxalate containing foods in my diet that day. Choosing organic guarantees these grains are not genetically modified. Genetically modified grains are engineered to withstand high amounts of herbicide and produce their own internal insecticide. With health on the line, it's best to err on the side of caution and stick with organic. Grains have a wide range of oxalate

contents. The recipes in this cookbook do not contain grains in the high oxalate range.

Legumes, Nuts and Seeds

Most legumes, nuts, and many seeds, are extremely high in oxalates. Lentils, coconut, and pumpkin seeds fall in the low oxalate range and can be found in many of my recipes.

FREE FOODS

You can find many oxalate food lists online created by some person, organization, or doctor, but they often have conflicting data. I created my list of oxalate free foods by examining as many lists as I could find and then eliminating any conflicting food item. For instance, if a food item was listed in any other category besides the oxalate free category, I eliminated it from my list of oxalate free foods simply as a precaution. These are the foods which I build my breakfasts, lunches, and snacks.

Beverages: Apple cider, water, chamomile tea, cherry juice, coconut water, and white wine.

Beans and Legumes: Black-eyed peas, green peas, and yellow split peas.

Condiments: Mustard, mayonnaise, vinegar.

Dairy: All dairy

Fats and Oils: Butter, coconut oil, and olive oil.

Fruits: Apples, avocados, bananas, cherries, cranberries, lemon, melons, nectarines, peaches, and plums.

Grains: White rice and barley.

Herbs and Spices: Basil, cilantro, mustard, nutmeg, white pepper, saffron, tarragon, vanilla, and sea salt.

Meats and Eggs: All meats and eggs.

Nuts and Seeds: Coconut, flax seeds, and pumpkin seeds.

Sweets & Sweeteners: White chocolate, raw sugar, maple syrup, honey.

Vegetables: Asparagus, broccoli, cabbages, cauliflower, corn, cucumbers, lettuces, mushrooms, mung bean sprouts, onions, radishes, sauerkraut, squash (zucchini, acorn, and yellow), red and yellow sweet peppers, turnips, and water chestnuts.

The hardest thing for me to change on the low oxalate diet was eliminating grain breads from my diet. Going gluten-free was not an option. Most gluten-free breads on the market contain high oxalate content foods: brown rice flour, potato starch, bean flour, oats or even worse, almond flour. I found it difficult to produce a good bread with low oxalate rice flour and coconut flour, although I do use them to make cookies or cakes. After trying many recipes for a gluten-free and oxalate free bread I finally stumbled upon a bread that's very popular in Brazil called Pao De Queijo. The main ingredients for these tasty cheese buns are tapioca starch and cheese. There are many different recipes for Pao De Queijo, and, after trying a few, I created my own much simpler version of this delicious cheese bread and called it

Tapioca Buns.

SERVES 6
INGREDIENTS
4 tbsp. (¼ cup) melted coconut oil
1 ½ cup tapioca flour (also known as tapioca starch)
1 tsp. baking powder
¼ tsp. salt
2 cups shredded cheese (parmesan or cheddar)
2 lg. eggs
1 tbsp. water

1. Preheat oven to 400 degrees.
2. Melt the coconut oil and set aside to cool.
3. In a large mixing bowl combine the tapioca flour, baking powder, and salt. (Careful, tapioca flour is very light and can be messy.)
4. Add the shredded cheese and mix well.
5. Add the eggs and the coconut oil. Mix it well with a fork at first and then by kneading. (It has to be worked really well with your hand. It may seem too dry, but you don't want it sticky.) Add 1 tbsp. of water if needed to form the dough.
6. Separate the dough into 6 equal sizes then shape each into rounds almost an inch thick.
7. Place them about an inch apart on a lightly oiled baking sheet.
8. Bake 400 degrees for 11-12 minutes. They will flatten out some and turn a very light brown. (If they get too brown they will be tough.)
9. Cool about 5 minutes before serving.

MY STORY

If you are looking for low oxalate meals you have probably been diagnosed with at least one of these conditions:

Kidney Stones
Fibromyalgia
Bladder Pain
Leaky Gut
Painful Joint Inflammation

I personally found myself in need of a low oxalate diet due to years of over consuming high oxalate foods on a daily basis. If your body does not get rid of the oxalates you are over-consuming in foods, these powerful and very reactive molecules can wreak havoc on your health.

Several years ago I was suddenly struck with debilitating shoulder joint pain. I could not raise my arm at all. Only ice would relieve the pain. Two days later, before a doctor appointment, the pain and inflammation was gone as if nothing had ever happened. After a few days this happened again in the other shoulder. Over and over this happened. Sometimes it would be a finger, sometimes my wrist. There was no medical explanation. Through prayer, God led me on a journey of discovery and finally, total healing.

A year before this happened; I had decided to change my diet. I took the traditional route and only ate fruits, vegetables, nuts, whole grains, and very lean meats. I practically eliminated dairy. I snacked on nuts several times a day and made sure to have spinach and sweet potatoes several times a week. I sprinkled cocoa in my morning coffee and my favorite fruits were blueberries and tangerines. Anyone who knows about oxalates would cringe at that diet.

I knew nothing about oxalates. One day I stumbled upon an article about oxalates in foods, and I began to study all of the information I could find. When I found the high oxalate food list and realized my entire diet was built on these high oxalate foods, I knew I had found some answers to my condition. I started a food diary to be sure. By examining the food diary I could easily see the relationship between the high oxalate foods I ate and the pain I would experience 36-48 hours later. I eliminated the foods with the highest oxalate content one week and then the medium level ones the next. Within weeks I was pain free. Then suddenly the horrible pain returned in my shoulders. Perplexed, I went online to talk to others with oxalate problems and learned about the danger of going low oxalate to quickly. I was going through what is called "dumping oxalates". It was debilitating. My back hurt so bad I thought it was an injury so I went to see a chiropractor. The first thing he did was an x-ray. We stood there looking at the x-ray, and he was very quiet. I was also looking at the small white spots showing on the x-ray around my shoulders and sprinkled all over my ribs thinking that was very odd looking. These turned out to be calcium oxalate crystals. The source of my pain. My steady diet of high oxalate foods had overwhelmed my system and caused my body to store the excess it could not excrete. When I stopped eating oxalate foods in the medium and high range my body had a chance to eliminate the stored oxalate crystals. A very painful process. Oxalate crystals are like tiny shards of glass. As they move they tear and inflame tissues. About eighty percent of kidney stones are caused by oxalates and they are by far the most common factor in kidney stone formation.

My road to health was long but successful. As my diet changed so did my health. Living low oxalate was a challenge the first year, but it's a way of life for me now. It's a powerful and effective program that addresses all oxalate issues in the body. By limiting my oxalate intake to 40-50 milligrams per day or less, as recommended by the National Kidney Foundation to prevent kidney stone flare ups, I've been pain free for years now.

Disclaimer: The recipes and views presented here are not intended as diagnosis, treatment, prescription or cure for any disease, mental or physical, and are not intended as a substitute for regular medical care. For diagnosis or treatment of any medical problem, consult your own physician. Always consult with your personal physician before beginning any new program or making any changes on your own. Any statements or claims about the health benefits conferred by any foods have not been evaluated by the FDA and are therefore not intended to diagnose, treat, cure or prevent any disease. The publisher and author are not responsible for any specific health needs and are not liable for any damages or negative consequences from any treatment, action, application or preparation, to any person reading or following the information in this book. The content of this book is the sole opinion of the author who is not in the medical profession therefore is not engaged to render any type of medical professional advice. The recipes and Cook's Notes reflect specifically on what has worked for the author.

BAKED LEMON ROSEMARY CHICKEN

Lemon and rosemary complement the richly roasted flavor of the chicken in this easy all-in-one dinner.

SERVES 4

INGREDIENTS

1 pound skinless, boneless, chicken breasts, cut 2 x 2 inch squares
2 small red potatoes, quartered
1 red pepper, sliced thick
1 large zucchini or yellow squash, sliced thick
1 large yellow or red onion, cut in 1 inch chunks
¼ cup olive oil
Juice of 1 lg. lemon
3 cloves fresh garlic, diced
½ tsp. salt
½ tsp. dried Italian spices
½ tsp. dried rosemary

1. Preheat oven to 425 degrees.
2. In a large 16 inch roasting pan, combine all of the ingredients and toss until all ingredients are well coated.
3. Bake 25-30 minutes. Turn on the broiler for the last 2-3 minutes to slightly brown the top.
4. Serve hot.

NUTRITIONAL INFORMATION			
Calories	225	Fat	14g
Carbohydrate	19g	Protein	7g

COOK'S NOTE
Rosemary is a fragrant herb with needle-like leaves that's known for having a wide array of health benefits. You have a winning immune boosting combination when you pair it with garlic and onions in a recipe.

CHICKEN CAESAR SALAD

Transform the classic Caesar into a main-course salad by topping it with seared chicken breasts, parmesan, and a fresh, bold, easy homemade Caesar dressing.

SERVES 2

INGREDIENTS
2 tbsp. coconut oil
2 boneless chicken breasts
1 large bunch romaine lettuce, chopped
Parmesan cheese (as topping)

Caesar Dressing
3 garlic cloves
½ cup extra virgin olive oil
¼ tsp Worcestershire sauce
2 tbsp. white wine vinegar
1 egg
1 tsp. dry mustard
¼ cup parmesan cheese, grated
¼ tsp. black pepper
4 anchovies

1. In a non-stick frying pan, heat oil over medium-high heat and place the chicken in the hot oil. Cook for 4 minutes.
2. Turn the chicken, and cook for 4 minutes more. Check if it's cooked by poking the tip of a sharp knife into the thickest part; there should be no sign of pink and juices will run clear. Set aside.
3. Place all of the dressing ingredients in a blender and blend until smooth.
4. Divide the romaine lettuce into 2 large bowls and pour equal amounts of dressing over each and toss to coat the leaves.
5. Place sliced chicken breasts on top of lettuce and garnish with cheese.

NUTRITIONAL INFORMATION			
Calories	342	Fat	7g
Carbohydrate	10g	Protein	58g

COOK'S NOTE
Bottled dressings today seem to be loaded with genetically modified soybean oil and high fructose corn syrup, which are two of the most harmful ingredients in foods. Once you've tried this Caesar dressing recipe you will never buy bottled Caesar dressing again.

CHICKEN GUMBO WITH EFFORTLESS ROUX

No need to be in the kitchen all day preparing this Cajun gumbo. The flavorful roux develops simply by frying the chicken in oil.

SERVES 4

INGREDIENTS

¼ cup flour
¼ tsp. salt
½ tsp. garlic powder
¼ tsp. white pepper
¼ tsp. cayenne pepper
1 lb. boneless chicken breasts or thighs, cut in 1 inch pieces
4 tbsp. coconut oil
1 medium red onion, chopped
5 medium tomatoes, chopped
1 tsp. dried basil
1 tsp. hot sauce (I prefer Tabasco due to the low salt content)
2 cups chicken broth or chicken bone broth
1 small zucchini, chopped
Cooked rice (optional)

1. In a medium-size mixing bowl combine the flour, salt, garlic, white pepper and cayenne.
2. Toss in the chicken pieces and coat each piece.
3. Heat 3 tbsp. oil in a large skillet over medium-high heat. (You want it hot enough to sizzle and turn the chicken strips a nice golden brown but not so hot that they'll burn easily.)
4. Brown and set aside. (The chicken doesn't have to be fully cooked at this time.)
5. In a large pot add the onion and the remaining oil (1 tbsp.) and cook over medium-high heat for 3 min. or until the onions have softened.
6. Add the chopped fresh tomatoes, basil, hot sauce, chicken broth and fried chicken pieces along with oil and drippings to the pot of onions.

7. Bring the gumbo to a boil over high heat and then reduce to a medium rolling simmer for 15 minutes. (Stir occasionally towards the end because it will begin to thicken.)
8. Add the chopped zucchini and continue to cook for another 10 minutes.
9. Serve in individual serving bowls or on top of rice.

NUTRITIONAL INFORMATION			
Calories	234	Fat	15g
Carbohydrate	15g	Protein	12g

COOK'S NOTE
With okra so high in oxalates it made me sad to think I had to give up a perfectly delicious bowl of gumbo. With one little tweak, adding diced zucchini near the end of the cooking time, I was surprised to find it added that same texture you get with okra. I was pleased to put gumbo back on my table again. The total time to prepare and cook this meal may be more than my 30 minute time preference, but it is well worth the effort.

CHICKEN LENTILS

Let your slow cooker do all of the work in this fragrant Indian dish seasoned with curry powder, ginger and garlic.

SERVES 2

INGREDIENTS
1 cup green or yellow lentils
½ tsp. curry powder
¼ tsp. cumin
¼ tsp. dry mustard
¼ tsp. dried cilantro
¼ tsp. white pepper
½ tsp. cayenne pepper
¼ tsp. dried ginger
2 cloves garlic, chopped
1 small red onion, chopped
1 medium tomato, chopped
3 cups chicken broth (can also use water)
2 boneless chicken breasts
Romaine or green leaf lettuce
1 small tomato, diced (optional)

1. Sort and rinse the lentils under warm water.
2. Place the first 12 ingredients in the bottom of a slow cooker and stir a little to mix the spices with the lentils.
3. Place the chicken breasts on top.
4. Cover and cook on low for 6-8 hours or on high for 3-4 hours.
5. Uncover and pull the chicken apart using 2 forks mixing the chicken into the lentils.
6. Serve in individual bowls with side salad or over romaine leaves and top with a small amount of diced tomato (optional).

NUTRITIONAL INFORMATION			
Calories	627	Fat	4g
Carbohydrate	64g	Protein	80g

COOK'S NOTE
Unlike most dried beans or legumes, lentils require no soaking before cooking. It's best to salt them after they are cooked because salt will toughen lentils if added during the cooking time. Lentils are a good source of magnesium and fiber.

FISH FRITTERS WITH SWEET & SPICY SAUCE

These savory fish fritters are paired smartly with the sweet and spicy dipping sauce.

SERVES 2-4

INGREDIENTS
1 pkg. (12 oz.) frozen mahi mahi fish fillets, thawed
½ cup water
1 tsp. lemon juice
½ cup cornmeal, plain
¼ cup flour, all purpose
1 tsp. baking powder
1 tsp. dried thyme
½ tsp. salt
½ tsp. cayenne pepper
¼ tsp. garlic powder
2 eggs, lightly beaten
2 tbsp. lemon juice
¼ medium red onion, finely chopped
¼ red bell pepper, finely chopped
3 tbsp. milk
½ cup coconut oil
1 avocado, sliced (optional)
1 tomato, sliced (optional)

SWEET & SPICY SAUCE
½ cup apricot jam
2 tbsp. water
3 tbsp. Dijon mustard
2 tbsp. lemon juice
½ tsp. cayenne pepper
¼ tsp. dried ginger
¼ tsp. red pepper flakes
¼ tsp. onion powder

1. Make the sweet and spicy sauce by adding all of the ingredients together. Mix well and set aside.
2. Simmer the fish in the water and lemon juice on high heat, for about 6 minutes, until the fish flakes easily. Drain and flake the fish into chunks then set aside.
3. In a large mixing bowl, combine the cornmeal, flour, baking powder, thyme, salt, cayenne and garlic. Mix well.

4. In another mixing bowl, lightly beat the eggs then add the lemon juice, onion, pepper and milk.
5. Add the wet ingredients to the dry ingredients and stir in the cooked fish. (Mix together really well.)
6. Heat oil in large skillet over medium-high heat. Form small (1 ½ inch) balls using a teaspoon and the palm of your hand and drop fritter mix in the hot oil.
7. Cook 1-2 minutes per side or until golden brown and drain on paper towels.
8. Serve fish fritters with the dipping sauce on the side and the sliced avocado and tomato if desired.

NUTRITIONAL INFORMATION			
Calories	359	Fat	16g
Carbohydrate	30g	Protein	23g

COOK'S NOTE
It's hard to imagine these super delicious fried fish fritters as healthy, but unlike typical restaurant fritters these are fried in unrefined coconut oil which promotes heart health, supports immune function, and helps maintain normal blood sugar levels.

GARDEN PASTA

A light, meatless, colorful pasta dish loaded with fresh vegetables and rich flavor.

SERVES 4

INGREDIENTS

Angel hair pasta (8 oz.) cooked according to package directions
1 medium red onion, sliced thinly
2 tbsp. butter
½ cup white wine
3 garlic cloves, chopped
½ tsp. salt
1 bunch (20-25 spears) asparagus, tough ends trimmed and cut into 1 inch pieces
½ zucchini, chopped
¼ cup extra virgin olive oil
1 roma tomato, diced
½ tsp. fresh basil, chopped
4 tbsp. sliced black olives, drained
½ cup parmesan cheese, grated or shredded

1. While the water for the pasta is coming to a boil stir-fry the onion in 1 tbsp. butter in a large skillet until soft.
2. Add the white wine, garlic, salt, and asparagus and cook for 4 minutes over medium heat. (This would be a good time to add the pasta to the boiling water.)
3. Add the zucchini and continue to cook for another 2 minutes.
4. Add the olive oil, 1 tbsp. butter, tomatoes, basil and olives and cook 2 minutes more.
5. Serve the garden mixture over the angel hair pasta and top with parmesan cheese.

NUTRITIONAL INFORMATION			
Calories	563	Fat	29g
Carbohydrate	51g	Protein	21g

COOK'S NOTE

This super quick dish delivers 83% of your daily requirement of Vitamin K. Vitamin K works with calcium and vitamin D to help move calcium into bones and teeth where it belongs instead of other areas of the body. It also keeps blood vessels from calcifying.

GROUND BEEF STIR-FRY

This quick and easy stir-fry dinner is delicious on its own, but I often serve it over white rice for a heartier meal.

SERVES 4-6

INGREDIENTS
1 lb. ground grass-fed beef (or turkey, venison, bison)
1 large red onion, chopped
½ red bell pepper, thinly sliced
½ tsp. salt
½ tsp. garlic powder
1 head Chinese (napa) cabbage, chopped
Cooked white rice (optional)

1. Brown beef in a large skillet or wok.
2. When the beef is almost completely browned add the onion, red pepper, salt and garlic.
3. When the onions have started to soften add the cabbage. (Add a small amount of water to steam the cabbage if it starts to stick to the skillet)
4. Cook about 2-3 minutes more, stirring often until the cabbage softens.
5. Serve as main dish or over rice.

NUTRITIONAL INFORMATION			
Calories	259	Fat	15g
Carbohydrate	8g	Protein	25g

COOK'S NOTE
This dish is a good source of B6, B12, potassium, and zinc.
You can vary this dish by adding seasonal vegetables, cutting them to a similar size in order to ensure that they cook in the same amount of time.

HERBED SALMON ON CREAMY PEA & CORN BED

Salmon with lavish sprinklings of mouthwatering spices served over a simple but elegant bed of creamy, colorful peas and corn.

SERVES 2

INGREDIENTS
1 lb. frozen or fresh, wild-caught Alaskan salmon filets
1 tbsp. butter
2 tbsp. Dijon mustard
½ tsp. basil
½ tsp. chives
½ tsp. thyme
½ tsp. dillweed
½ tsp. garlic powder
½ tsp. salt
½ tsp. white pepper

Creamy Pea & Corn Bed
1 tbsp. butter
1 cup frozen sweet peas
1 cup frozen sweet corn
¾ cup whole milk
1 garlic clove, crushed
1 tsp. dried thyme

1. Preheat oven to 425 degrees.
2. Place salmon in a buttered 9" x 13" baking pan or dish, skin side down.
3. Coat each salmon filet with Dijon mustard.
4. Combine the basil, chives, thyme, dillweed, garlic, salt and pepper in a small bowl and sprinkle over the salmon filets.
5. Roast 15-18 minutes, without turning.
6. While the salmon fillets are cooking add the remaining ingredients to a medium-size saucepan and cook over medium-high heat (simmering) until cream is reduced by one-third and slightly thickened. (This will take about 6-7 minutes after reaching a boil.)
7. To serve, place a generous mound of creamy pea and corn in the middle of each plate. Spread it out so that it creates a bed for the salmon. Place a fillet of salmon on top.

NUTRITIONAL INFORMATION			
Calories	604	Fat	30g
Carbohydrate	32g	Protein	53g

COOK'S NOTE
The salmon seasonings are an excellent source of phytochemicals which fend off damaging free radicals. These salmon filets can be grilled in the summer months for an even greater flavor.

JAMAICAN JERK THIGHS

These tender, dry-rubbed, spicy jerk chicken thighs will capture your taste buds.

SERVES 4

INGREDIENTS
1 tbsp. allspice
1 tsp. onion powder
1 tsp. ground ginger
½ tsp. white pepper
½ tsp. dried thyme
½ tsp. salt
¼ tsp. nutmeg
1 tsp. cayenne pepper
6-8 boneless, skinless, chicken thighs
Cooked rice
Sliced tomatoes (optional)

1. Preheat oven to 425 degrees.
2. Mix the first 8 spices in a small bowl.
3. Coat the chicken thighs in spices and place in a lightly oiled baking dish. (I use a glass casserole dish.)
4. Bake for 25 minutes. (Boneless chicken thighs cook quickly.)
5. For very tender chicken, cover the baking dish with foil and let the chicken rest for about 5 minutes. Roll thighs in the drippings and serve.
6. Excellent served over rice using the drippings as gravy.

NUTRITIONAL INFORMATION			
Calories	128	Fat	3g
Carbohydrate	9g	Protein	15g

COOK'S NOTE
Allspice is the main ingredient in Jamaican jerk seasoning. It's known for having many health benefits including an anti-inflammatory effect. Bone-in chicken thighs can be used as well, but they will require an additional 20 minutes cooking time and will need to be turned at least once.

LOADED BEEF BURGER

A thick vegetable puree adds both moisture and nutrients to these grass-fed beef burgers.

SERVES 4-6
INGREDIENTS
½ small zucchini, cut in 4 pieces
1 small red onion, quartered
½ small red or yellow sweet pepper, quartered
1 cup broccoli florets
2 garlic cloves
1 egg
1 lb. ground grass-fed beef (or turkey, venison, bison)
¼ tsp. salt
Hamburger buns (I prefer Tapioca Buns. Recipe on Page 13.)

1. Preheat oven to 375 degrees.
2. Puree the zucchini, onion, red sweet pepper, broccoli and garlic in a food processor or blender.
3. In a large bowl combine the pureed vegetable and the remaining ingredients.
4. Form patties (6) and place on a large baking sheet with raised sides, to keep any juices from spilling over into the oven. (Unlike a traditional burger these will not shrink up very much so you will want to shape them bun size.)
5. Bake uncovered, for 25-30 minutes or until meat is no longer pink.
6. Serve on buns with your favorite toppings.

NUTRITIONAL INFORMATION			
Calories	274	Fat	17g
Carbohydrate	6g	Protein	26g

COOK'S NOTE
Baked, fried, or grilled these vegetable loaded burgers are delicious and highly nutritious. They are a good source of calcium, zinc, and vitamin B6.

LO-OX CHILI

This spicy, savory, off-beat chili is packed with nutrition as well as flavor.

SERVES 4-6

INGREDIENTS
1 tbsp. coconut oil
1 lb. ground grass-fed beef (or turkey, venison, bison)
1 red onion, chopped
1 small red bell pepper, chopped
3 garlic cloves, minced
1 tsp. ground cumin
1 tbsp. chili powder
½ tsp. cayenne pepper
3 cups tomatoes, diced
1 tsp. dried basil
16 ounce pkg. frozen black-eyed peas
1 ½ cups water
1 cup pumpkin puree
Salt & pepper (as desired after cooking)
Optional toppings: sour cream or shredded cheddar cheese

1. Cook the first 8 ingredients in a large saucepan over medium-high heat, stirring often, until meat crumbles and is no longer pink.
2. Add diced tomatoes, basil, peas, water, and pumpkin to the beef mixture.
3. Bring to a boil over high heat then reduce heat to medium for 30 minutes. (Sustain a rolling simmer and stir occasionally.)
4. Serve in soup bowls with desired toppings.

NUTRITIONAL INFORMATION				
Calories	522		Fat	16g
Carbohydrate	62g		Protein	37g

COOK'S NOTE
Adding salt to peas as they cook will result in tough peas. If salt is desired, add it just before serving. Black-eyed peas are on the very low oxalates
foods list making them the perfect "bean" for most recipes. They are especially high in potassium and zinc, which is important for the proper function of all cells.

MAHI MAHI WITH ARTICHOKE HEARTS

Packed full of flavor, this delicious fish dish is a meal in itself but can be accompanied by rice.

SERVES 2

INGREDIENTS
1 tsp. red pepper flakes
¼ tsp. salt
¼ tsp. white pepper
1 ½ tbsp. all purpose flour
4 tbsp. butter (2 tbsp. for frying and 2 tbsp. added later)
1 pkg. (12 oz.) frozen mahi mahi fish fillets, thawed and patted dry
Juice of ½ lemon
2 tbsp. heavy whipping cream
¼ tsp. dried basil
1 garlic clove, pressed
12 oz. jar artichoke hearts, drained and rinsed
4-5 oz. sun-dried tomatoes in olive oil, drained but not rinsed
Cooked rice (optional)

1. On a large plate add the red pepper flakes, salt and pepper to the flour then spread it out.
2. In a large non-stick frying pan, melt 2 tbsp. butter over moderate heat.
3. Dust the fish with a small amount of flour and shake off any excess.
4. Cook fish on one side to a light golden brown (about 3-4 minutes) then turn and cook an additional 3-4 minutes lowering the heat to medium.
5. Add the remaining butter (2 tbsp.) lemon juice, heavy whipping cream, basil and garlic.
6. Blend and spoon it over the fish then add the artichoke hearts and the sun-dried tomatoes.
7. Cook only a minute or two more stirring the artichokes and tomatoes into the lemon butter sauce.

8. Place the fish on plates, top with the artichoke, tomatoes, and lemon butter sauce.
9. For a fuller meal serve over rice.

NUTRITIONAL INFORMATION			
Calories	642	Fat	37g
Carbohydrate	43g	Protein	42g

COOK'S NOTE
Grouper could be an alternative to mahi mahi as both of these fish are firm and flavorful. Each serving provides 41% of your daily requirements for B6 and magnesium.

ORIENTAL SOUP

An exotic soup with the perfect blend of sweet and spice.

SERVES 4-6

INGREDIENTS
1 tbsp. coconut oil
1 red onion, chopped
2 boneless chicken breasts, cut into small cubes
3 garlic cloves, crushed
½ tsp. ginger
½ tsp. salt
½ tsp. white pepper
1 tsp. red pepper flakes
2 tsp. chives
2 cups chicken or bone broth
1 head Chinese (napa) or savoy cabbage, chopped
1 ½ cups coconut milk
1 (8 oz.) can bamboo shoots, drained and rinsed
1 (8 oz.) can sliced water chestnuts, drained and rinsed
1 (14 oz.) can bean sprouts (mung beans), drained and rinsed

1. Melt the oil in a large saucepan over high heat.
2. Add the onion and saute until soft.
3. Add the chicken, garlic, ginger, salt, peppers, and chives and continue to stir until chicken is no longer pink inside.
4. Pour in the broth and then add the cabbage.
5. Continue to cook over high heat, for about 10 minutes, until the cabbage is tender.
6. Pour in the coconut milk, bamboo shoots, water chestnuts, and bean sprouts.
7. Let it return to a boil then reduce the heat and simmer for about 5 more minutes.
8. Transfer soup to individual soup bowls and serve hot.

NUTRITIONAL INFORMATION			
Calories	380	Fat	20g
Carbohydrate	24g	Protein	29g

COOK'S NOTE
Oriental vegetables like bamboo shoots, water chestnuts, and bean sprouts have impressive health benefits. These fiber rich vegetables are loaded with antioxidants, vitamins, and minerals that strengthen the immune system.

PIZZA CASSEROLE

This recipe is more like a deep dish pizza with an amazing flourless crust.

SERVES 4-6

INGREDIENTS
CRUST
4 oz. cream cheese, softened
2 eggs
¼ tsp. Italian seasoning
¼ tsp. garlic powder
¼ cup parmesan cheese (1 oz.)
8 oz. mozzarella cheese, shredded

TOPPINGS
1 red onion, diced
1 lb. ground grass-fed beef
3 cups spaghetti sauce (I prefer Eden Organic or Muir Glen Organic)
4 ounces mozzarella cheese, shredded
Additional toppings: mushrooms, red peppers, olives

1. Preheat oven to 400 degrees.
2. In a medium-size bowl, blend the softened cream cheese with the eggs, Italian seasonings, and garlic until smooth and creamy.
3. Stir in the parmesan and mozzarella until it's all moistened.
4. Spread the crust mixture evenly in a well oiled, 9x13 inch glass or ceramic baking dish.
5. Bake 20-25 minutes until evenly browned.
6. Stir-fry the diced onion and ground beef.
7. Top the crust with cooked ground beef and the spaghetti sauce and any additional toppings. Top with the mozzarella cheese.
8. Bake at 400 degrees for about 5 minutes or until the cheese is melted.
9. Let stand a few minutes before cutting.

NUTRITIONAL INFORMATION			
Calories	831	Fat	54g
Carbohydrate	33g	Protein	54g

COOK'S NOTE
One serving of this deep dish pizza supplies 78% of your daily requirement for Vitamin B12 and 43% of your daily requirement for Vitamin B6.

SALMON PASTA CASSEROLE

A rich and hearty meal full of calcium and omega-3 fatty acids.

SERVES 4
INGREDIENTS
3 cups cooked (according to package directions) rice noodles (I prefer Pad Thai Rice Noodles)
1 cup broccoli florets
1 cup frozen sweet peas
1 can (14 oz.) wild-caught salmon, drained
2 eggs
1 tbsp. lemon juice
2 medium green onions
1 cup plain whole milk yogurt
1 cup cheddar cheese, shredded

1. Preheat oven to 350 degrees.
2. Cook rice noodles according to package directions along with the broccoli florets and peas.
3. Drain the pasta, peas and broccoli and set aside.
4. In a large mixing bowl, flake the salmon and mix it with the eggs and lemon juice; and then stir in the green onions, yogurt, and cheese.
5. Lightly oil a 9x13 casserole dish.
6. Layer the dish with the cooked pasta, peas, and broccoli and top with salmon mix.
7. Bake for 20 minutes. (It will start to bubble round the edges and turn a golden color. You don't want to let it go too dark, the fish will overcook.)

NUTRITIONAL INFORMATION			
Calories	469	Fat	19g
Carbohydrate	45g	Protein	29g

COOK'S NOTE
Pad Thai noodles are a great replacement for wheat pasta in this salmon pasta casserole. The texture and flavor are very similar. Canned salmon is calcium rich, provides high quality protein, and is an omega-3 powerhouse.

SALMON PATTIES WITH EASY CHEESY ASPARAGUS

Fast and fabulous salmon patties topped with asparagus in a delightful cream cheese sauce.

SERVES 4
INGREDIENTS
Easy Cheesy Asparagus
1 bunch (25-30 stalks) fresh asparagus, ends trimmed and cut into 2 inch pieces
1 cup water
1 tbsp. lemon juice
1 tbsp. butter
1 garlic clove, minced
4 oz. cream cheese
¼ tsp. salt
⅓ cup milk

Salmon Patties
1 can (14 ¾ oz.) wild Alaskan salmon, well drained
2 green onions, chopped
¼ tsp. dried dill
1 tsp. lemon juice
1 tbsp. Dijon mustard
1 garlic clove, minced
1 egg
¼ tsp. salt
¼ tsp. white pepper
3 tbsp. coconut oil

1. In a medium-size saucepan bring the asparagus, water, and lemon to a boil over high heat. Turn down to medium heat and simmer for about 3 minutes.
2. Combine the drained salmon, onions, dill, lemon, Dijon, garlic, egg, salt and pepper in a large mixing bowl. Mix well.
3. In a large skillet, heat oil over medium-high heat.

4. Form golf ball size balls then flatten a little after placing them in the heated oil. (Makes 6 patties.)
5. Cook patties until browned on one side, for about 4-5 minutes, then carefully turn and brown on the other side. Remove to drain on paper towels.
6. Drain the water off of the asparagus and add butter, garlic, cream cheese, and salt. Continue to cook over medium heat, stirring often, until the cheese is melted.
7. Stir the milk into to the melted cheese and asparagus, and cook another minute stirring often.
8. Serve the salmon patties topped with cheesy asparagus.

NUTRITIONAL INFORMATION			
Calories	361	Fat	25g
Carbohydrate	8g	Protein	29g

COOK'S NOTE
Choose wild-caught Alaskan salmon over farm-raised to avoid toxins and antibiotics.

SEARED MAHI MAHI SALAD

A refreshing light meal packed with flavor and nutrition. Pan-seared mahi mahi is an easy to cook firm, delicate flavored fish.

SERVES 2
INGREDIENTS
Dressing
½ tsp. dried basil
¼ tsp. hot sauce (I prefer Tabasco due to the low salt content)
1 tbsp. balsamic vinaigrette
½ tsp. honey
1 tbsp. extra virgin olive oil
Salad
1 packed cup arugula
½ cup cherry or golden snack tomatoes, halved
1 large tomato, chopped
2 cups arugula
1 large radish, sliced into thin strips
Fish
1 ½ tbsp. all purpose flour
1 tsp. red pepper flakes
¼ tsp. salt
¼ tsp. white pepper
2 tbsp. coconut oil
1 pkg. (12 oz.) frozen mahi mahi fillets thawed and patted dry. (Can substitute with grouper, snapper or sea bass)

1. Blend the first 5 ingredients together for the dressing and set aside.
2. Prepare the salad ingredients and divide onto 2 plates.
3. On a large plate combine the flour, the red pepper flakes, salt and pepper.
4. Add coconut oil to a hot skillet.
5. Dredge both sides of the fish in the flour.

6. Cook fish on one side to a light golden brown, for about 3-4 minutes, then turn and cook an additional 3-4 minutes lowering the heat to medium.
7. Place the fish in the center of each salad plate.
8. Drizzle the salad with dressing and serve immediately.

NUTRITIONAL INFORMATION			
Calories	420	Fat	18g
Carbohydrate	20g	Protein	43g

COOK'S NOTE
Fish is one of the healthiest foods you can eat. The good fat and protein has been shown to fight heart disease, boost brain health and improve skin and hair. However, these benefits can be canceled out if it's contaminated with antibiotics or chemicals. Avoid farmed fish by looking for the words "wild-caught" on the fish packaging.

SLOW COOKER BARBECUE CHICKEN

This shredded barbecue chicken will become a lean and healthy favorite. This easy homemade barbecue sauce is so delicious you will never be tempted to buy barbecue sauce again.

SERVES 4

INGREDIENTS
1 tbsp. coconut oil
2 boneless chicken breasts
1 cup organic ketchup (without high fructose corn syrup)
¼ cup honey
1 tbsp. apple cider vinegar
2 tbsp. Worcestershire sauce
½ cup water
2 tsp. mustard
3 garlic cloves, crushed
½ tsp. paprika
½ tsp. onion powder
½ tsp. white pepper
½ tsp. sea salt
Cooked rice or buns

1. Spread the oil in the bottom of the slow cooker then add the chicken breasts.
2. In a bowl, mix remaining ingredients and pour over the chicken.
3. Cook on low 6-8 hours or on high for 3-4 hours.
4. Shred the chicken with forks when done and mix well with the sauce.
5. Serve over rice or on a bun. (I prefer Tapioca Buns. Recipe on Page 13.)

NUTRITIONAL INFORMATION			
Calories	281	Fat	5g
Carbohydrate	32g	Protein	28g

COOK'S NOTE
Chicken breasts fall apart into easy threads. Another option would be to use boneless chicken thighs.

SLOW COOKER CHICKEN GARDEN PASTA

This light and nutritious version of chicken spaghetti is flavorful and satisfying. Perfect when you are craving comfort food but want to maintain a healthy diet.

SERVES 4

INGREDIENTS
1 small red onion, chopped
½ red pepper, chopped
1 garlic clove, crushed
1 bunch (20-25 spears) asparagus, tough ends trimmed and cut into 1" pieces
2 cups fresh broccoli florets
½ cup water
1 boneless chicken breast
8 oz spaghetti pasta
2 medium zucchini, shredded
Parmesan cheese (as desired)

1. Cover the bottom of the slow cooker with the onions, peppers, and garlic and then top with asparagus and broccoli.
2. Add the water and the boneless chicken breast.
3. Cook on low for 6-8 hours or on high for 3-4 hours.
4. Just before serving, cook the spaghetti according to package directions.
5. While the spaghetti is cooking, pull apart the chicken breast and stir all of the slow cooker ingredients together.
6. Shred the zucchini into a small saucepan adding just enough water to cover it. Heat to a boil then remove from heat and drain the liquid.
7. Layer the dish with pasta, zucchini, the slow cooked vegetable and chicken mix. Garnish with parmesan cheese.

NUTRITIONAL INFORMATION			
Calories	417	Fat	13g
Carbohydrate	51g	Protein	28g

COOK'S NOTE
This is a variation of the traditional chicken spaghetti. It's loaded with energy boosting vegetables that go nicely together.

SLOW COOKER INDIAN CHICKEN

A simple and exquisite Indian dish. In India this is made with goat meat. Lamb or pork would work as well, but chicken is preferred in my home.

SERVES 4-6

INGREDIENTS
1 red onion, thinly sliced
½ red bell pepper, chopped
3 garlic cloves, thinly sliced
2 boneless chicken breasts
1 head Chinese (napa) cabbage, chopped
½ tsp. ginger
1 tsp. curry powder
¼ tsp. cayenne pepper
¼ tsp. white pepper
¼ tsp. salt
1 can (13 oz.) coconut milk
1½ cups chicken broth
Cooked rice

1. Spread the onions, red pepper, and garlic around the bottom of the slow cooker.
2. Place the chicken over the onion mix.
3. Add the chopped cabbage and the 5 seasonings.
4. Pour the coconut milk and the chicken broth over the cabbage and with a large spoon press down the ingredients.
5. Cook on high for 4-6 hours.
6. Using two forks shred the chicken and mix the ingredients.
7. Serve over rice.

NUTRITIONAL INFORMATION			
Calories	359	Fat	20g
Carbohydrate	13g	Protein	34g

COOK'S NOTE
All of the flavors come through in a balanced way in this slow approach to making a traditional Indian dish that includes curry powder. Research suggests curry powder may help remove metals like lead and mercury from the body.

SLOW COOKER MEATLOAF MEAL

Moist with mixed vegetables, this meatloaf still retains it's shape in the slow cooker. The meat juices mingle with the potatoes making them absolutely delicious.

SERVES 4-6
INGREDIENTS
½ head cauliflower florets
½ red or yellow pepper, quartered
½ tsp. salt
½ tsp. white pepper
1 garlic clove
1 red onion, chopped
1 cup pumpkin puree
2 eggs, slightly beaten
1 lb. ground grass-fed beef (or turkey, venison, bison)
2-3 red potatoes, halved
Ketchup*
Fresh basil, chopped as garnish

1. Using a food processor or blender, add cauliflower, red or yellow pepper, salt, pepper, and garlic. Process until the ingredients are pureed.
2. In a large bowl, combine the pureed vegetables, chopped onion, pumpkin, eggs, and ground beef. Mix well.
3. Tear off a sheet of aluminum foil large enough to cover the bottom and sides of the slow cooker and place in the cooker. Not only will it help you shape a good loaf, but it will make removing it easy.
4. Spoon the loaf into the slow cooker and shape by gathering the aluminum foil ends and bouncing it a bit.
5. Pull each side of the foil toward the center and place the potatoes around both sides of the slow cooker.
6. Move foil back to the sides and top the meatloaf with ketchup.
7. Cover and cook on high for 6-8 hours.

8. Easily remove the meatloaf by lifting the aluminum foil then transfer it to a serving dish.
9. Arrange the potatoes around the meatloaf and garnish with chopped fresh basil.

NUTRITIONAL INFORMATION			
Calories	253	Fat	11g
Carbohydrate	20g	Protein	19g

COOK'S NOTE
This fabulous vegetable loaded meatloaf is a good source of vitamin B6, B12, and zinc.
*Avoid ketchup that contains high fructose corn syrup.

SLOW COOKER TAMALE PIE

A little tweak on the classic southwestern comfort food. This rich, warming meal tastes like the authentic Mexican tamale but without all of the work.

SERVES 4

INGREDIENTS
1 lb. ground grass-fed beef (or turkey, venison, bison)
1 medium red onion, chopped
1 tbsp. chili powder
1 tsp. cumin
3 cups spaghetti sauce (I prefer Eden Organic or Muir Glen Organic)
2-4 tbsp. olives, minced or sliced
2 cups corn
2 eggs, beaten
1 cup milk
2 tbsp. olive oil
1 ¼ cup yellow cornmeal, plain
1 tsp. baking powder
1 tsp. baking soda
½ tsp. salt
1 cup cheddar or monterey jack cheese

1. In a large mixing bowl combine the ground beef, onion, chili powder and cumin. Then press the meat mixture into the bottom of the slow cooker.
2. Pour the spaghetti sauce over the meat
3. Sprinkle the olives over the sauce and add the corn on top.
4. Mix the egg, milk and oil together; then add the cornmeal, baking powder, baking soda and salt. Mix and pour batter over the corn.
5. Cook on high for 4-6 hours.
6. Sprinkle the cheese on top and let it melt a few minutes before serving.

NUTRITIONAL INFORMATION			
Calories	756	Fat	33g
Carbohydrate	82g	Protein	36g

COOK'S NOTE
One serving of this flavor packed tamale pie delivers 48% of your daily requirement for B6, 32% of your daily requirement for potassium, and 24% of your daily requirement for magnesium.

SLOW COOKER UNSTUFFED CABBAGE

Easy, delicious, healthy, and without all of the work that goes into making the traditional stuffed cabbage roll.

SERVES 4

INGREDIENTS

1 lb. ground grass-fed beef (or turkey, venison, bison)
1 cup uncooked rice
1 medium red onion, finely chopped
1 medium red or yellow pepper, finely chopped
I medium green or purple cabbage, chopped
4 roma tomatoes, chopped
1 jar tomato or spaghetti sauce (I prefer Eden Organic or Muir Glen)
½ cup water
1 tsp. salt
½ tsp. white pepper

1. Stir-fry the beef over medium-high heat and add to the slow cooker.
2. Add the remaining ingredients to the slow cooker in the order written.
3. Cook on low for 6-8 hours or on high for 3-4 hours.
4. Stir the pot and serve hot.

NUTRITIONAL INFORMATION			
Calories	579	Fat	18g
Carbohydrate	75g	Protein	31g

COOK'S NOTE
Cabbage is a superfood chock-full of antioxidants and sulfur-based compounds called glucosinolates, which protects one from developing a leaky gut. A leaky gut has been linked to oxalate issues in the body.

STEAK & BRUSSELS SPROUT HASH

An elegant but simple meal with skillet seared ribeye steak, Brussels sprouts, and potatoes.

SERVES 2

INGREDIENTS
2 red potatoes, peeled and cut in chunks
6 oz. fresh or thawed Brussels sprouts
1 medium red onion, chopped
2 garlic cloves, sliced
2 tbsp. butter
2 small ribeye steaks
½ tsp. salt
½ tsp. white pepper
¼ cup dry white wine such as Pinot Grigio

1. Prepare potatoes and Brussels sprouts. In a medium-size saucepan cover them with water and bring to a boil. Reduce to medium heat and simmer until tender when pierced (7-8 minutes). Drain and set aside when done.
2. While the potatoes and Brussels sprouts are cooking, prepare the onion and garlic and set aside.
3. Heat the butter in a large skillet over high heat.
4. Add salt and pepper to the dried steaks and sear both sides in the hot skillet.
5. Add the onion and garlic to the skillet; reduce to a medium-high heat and cover.
6. Cook covered, 2-3 minutes, until the onions have browned.
7. Remove the steaks to individual plates.
8. Add the drained Brussels sprouts, potatoes and the wine to the skillet and cook about 1 minute, stirring occasionally to scrape up any caramelized bits from bottom of pan.
9. Serve the hash over the seared ribeye steaks.

NUTRITIONAL INFORMATION			
Calories	606	Fat	21g
Carbohydrate	42g	Protein	57g

COOK'S NOTE
Brussels sprouts are one of the world's healthiest foods. They are a good source of iron, potassium, and folate. Brussels sprouts pair well with beef due to the high levels of other B vitamins in the beef. B vitamins work together to release energy from food.

SUPERFOOD SOUP

A delicious, thick and hearty soup that is rich in flavor and nutrition.

SERVES 4

INGREDIENTS
1 tbsp. coconut oil
1 red onion, chopped
3 garlic cloves, chopped
1 red bell pepper, chopped
1 head Chinese (napa) cabbage, chopped
4 cups chicken stock or bone broth
1 head fresh cauliflower florets, cut in 1 inch pieces
1 ½ cups pumpkin puree
½ tsp. ginger
½ tsp. cayenne
¼ tsp. nutmeg
1 tsp. salt
1 tsp. white pepper
1 cup raw pumpkin seeds (optional)

1. In a large soup pot, over medium-high heat, heat the oil and saute the onions, garlic and red bell peppers for 2 minutes.
2. Add the Napa cabbage and cook for one minute, stirring consistently.
3. Add the broth and cauliflower and bring to a boil, then reduce the heat to medium and simmer, stirring occasionally, for 25 minutes.
4. Blend in the pumpkin puree, ginger, cayenne, nutmeg, salt and pepper.
5. Serve in soup bowls topped with raw pumpkin seeds (optional).

NUTRITIONAL INFORMATION			
Calories	206	Fat	7g
Carbohydrate	28g	Protein	11g

COOK'S NOTE
This thick and creamy soup is packed with nutrition and flavor. Each serving supplies 33% of your daily requirement for vitamin B6, 32% of your daily requirement for vitamin K and 32% of your daily requirement for potassium. Topping your soup with pumpkin seeds is a great way to add zinc and vitamin E as well.

SWEET & SPICY STIR-FRY

A quick and easy stir-fry with a delicate sweet flavor.

SERVES 2

INGREDIENTS
2 tbsp. coconut oil
½ red onion, thinly sliced
½ red bell pepper, thinly sliced
1 lg. boneless chicken breast filet, cut into ¾ inch pieces
2 garlic cloves, crushed
¼ tsp. dried ginger
½ tsp. cayenne pepper
½ tsp. white pepper
1 head Chinese (napa) or savoy cabbage
4 tbsp. rice wine (may substitute with any dry white wine)
¼ cup apricot jam
Cooked rice (optional)

1. Heat the wok or skillet over high heat and add the coconut oil.
2. When the oil is heated, add onion and bell pepper and cook until tender.
3. Add the cut up chicken and stir-fry for about 3 minutes. (Cut a piece to make sure it's not pink inside.)
4. Season with garlic, ginger, cayenne, and white pepper.
5. Add the cabbage and continue to stir-fry, about 8 minutes, until it starts to brown and stick to the skillet.
6. Reduce the heat to medium-high. Add the wine and the apricot jam and stir-fry for another minute to blend the flavors.
7. Transfer to a serving dish, and serve hot or over cooked rice for a fuller meal.

NUTRITIONAL INFORMATION			
Calories	221	Fat	8g
Carbohydrate	20g	Protein	17g

COOK'S NOTE
Stir-frying is a fast, easy, and healthy way to cook. It's a good idea to measure and cut up ingredients before you heat the wok or skillet.

TACO SALAD

No seasoning packets needed in this simple taco salad recipe. A fast and flavorful southwestern meal.

SERVES 4
INGREDIENTS
½ small red onion, chopped
½ red bell pepper, chopped
1 tsp. coconut oil
1 lb. ground grass-fed beef
3 tbsp. water
1 garlic clove, crushed
1 tsp. dried cilantro
1 ½ tsp. dried cumin
½ tsp. salt
½ tsp. white pepper
1 large head romaine lettuce, chopped
10 tortilla chips, crushed
¼ cup olives, sliced
2 tomatoes, chopped
1 cup (4 ounces) cheddar cheese, shredded
4 tbsp. plain whole milk yogurt or sour cream
1 cup salsa (optional)

1. In a large non-stick skillet over high heat cook the onion and bell pepper in the oil until soft.
2. Add the beef, water, garlic, cilantro, cumin, salt and pepper and stir-fry until the meat is browned.
3. Place 1 cup lettuce on each of the 4 plates and top each with crumbled chips and 4 ounces of beef.
4. Sprinkle each serving with olives, tomato, and cheese.
5. Top with plain whole milk yogurt or sour cream.
6. Add salsa if desired.

NUTRITIONAL INFORMATION			
Calories	448	Fat	28g
Carbohydrate	18g	Protein	34g

COOK'S NOTE
Avoid processed foods and make your own taco salad at home. I prefer Simply Tostitos® Blue Corn Chips by Frito Lay because they are made with certified organic corn cooked in expeller pressed sunflower oil. There are no preservatives, artificial flavors or colors in this product.

TURKEY SAUSAGE CASSEROLE

An easy and incredibly delicious breakfast for dinner meal.

SERVES 4

INGREDIENTS

1 lb. ground turkey (grass fed-beef is another option)
1 tbsp. Dijon mustard
½ tsp. sage
½ tsp. rosemary
¼ tsp. salt
½ tsp. cayenne pepper
½ tsp. white pepper
½ tsp. garlic powder
¼ tsp. cumin
¼ tsp. chili powder
¼ tsp. fennel
½ medium red onion, diced
1 medium zucchini, shredded.
5 eggs
1 ½ cup Italian blend shredded cheese

1. Preheat oven to 375 degrees.
2. In a large mixing bowl combine the ground turkey, mustard, sage, rosemary, salt, cayenne pepper, white pepper, garlic powder, cumin, chili powder and fennel to make the sausage. Mix well.
3. Saute the sausage and onion over high heat until browned.
4. Add the zucchini and cook a minute more.
5. In a separate mixing bowl beat the eggs and stir in the cheese.
6. Mix the egg and cheese with the browned sausage and pour into a lightly buttered 9x13 casserole dish.
7. Bake for 20 minutes.
8. Cool for 5 minutes before serving.

NUTRITIONAL INFORMATION			
Calories	587	Fat	41g
Carbohydrate	5g	Protein	49g

COOK'S NOTE
Say goodbye to all those food additives and make your own turkey sausage. You'll never go back to buying ready-made again. The sausage can also be made into patties or sausage balls.

VEGETABLE EGG STIR-FRY

This blend of fresh vegetables with eggs is delicious over shredded romaine lettuce for a meal in minutes.

SERVES 2

INGREDIENTS
1 cup romaine, shredded
1 small red onion, chopped
½ red pepper, chopped
2 tbsp. butter
½ bunch (10-15 spears) asparagus, tough ends trimmed and cut into 1 inch pieces
⅓ cup water
1 medium zucchini, shredded
5 eggs, beaten
1 small tomato, chopped
1 avocado, peeled and chopped
½ cup cheddar cheese, shredded
Cayenne pepper (optional)

1. Divide the shredded romaine onto 2 plates.
2. Over medium-high heat, stir-fry the onion and pepper in the butter until soft.
3. Add the asparagus and water. Cook about 3 minutes.
4. Add the shredded zucchini and cook an additional 2-3 minutes.
5. Pour in the beaten eggs and stir often until cooked soft.
6. Remove from heat and spoon over romaine lettuce.
7. Add the chopped tomato and avocado
8. Top with cheese and cayenne pepper.

NUTRITIONAL INFORMATION			
Calories	698	Fat	50g
Carbohydrate	39g	Protein	34g

COOK'S NOTE
Eggs contain high quality proteins, fats, vitamins and minerals. Pair them with vegetables for a powerful combination of antioxidant nutrients.

VERY VEGGIE SPAGHETTI

Shredded zucchini replaces the pasta in this healthier grain-free and vegetable packed version of spaghetti.

SERVES 2

INGREDIENTS
2 zucchini, shredded
¼ small red onion
½ red bell pepper
2 cloves garlic
4 roma tomatoes, halved
½ tsp. basil
½ tsp. oregano
½ tsp. salt
1 tbsp. extra virgin olive oil
¼ cup parmesan cheese

1. Shred the zucchini in a food processor or use a cheese grater.
2. In a medium-size saucepan cover the zucchini with water and bring to a boil then remove from heat. Let it stand as you prepare the sauce.
3. Add the onion, red bell pepper, garlic, tomatoes, basil, oregano and salt to your blender or food processor and puree until smooth.
4. Heat the oil in a medium-size saucepan or skillet and add the vegetable puree. Cook for 5-6 minutes over medium-high heat.
5. Drain the zucchini.
6. Serve the sauce over the zucchini.
7. Top with parmesan cheese.

NUTRITIONAL INFORMATION			
Calories	178	Fat	11g
Carbohydrate	20g	Protein	5g

COOK'S NOTE
The latest noodle trend is actually a vegetable. Whether you use zucchini or spaghetti squash, you can turn your high-carb pasta dishes into light and healthy versions.

Find More Low Oxalate Recipes in *Real Food Real Results*

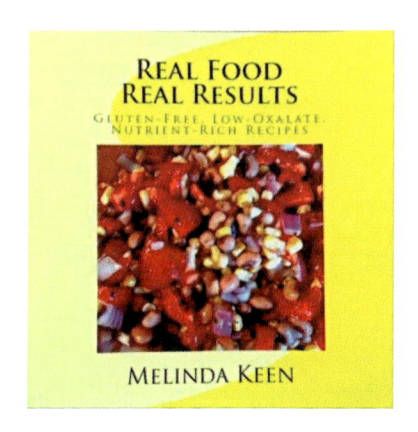

ISBN-10: 1517478537
ISBN-13: 978-1517478537

Optimal health, vibrant energy, and ideal weight can be achieved with real food nutrition. Nutrition with real food is eating organic real foods and removing processed and refined foods as well as foods responsible for allergies and autoimmune disease. Building on the success of her first cookbook, *Low Oxalate Fresh and Fast Cookbook* (2015) Melinda Keen announces her second cookbook, **Real Food Real Results: Gluten-Free, Low-Oxalate, Nutrient-Rich Recipes**, featuring over 50 new recipes that are not only nutrient-rich but gluten-free and low in oxalates as well. This original collection includes recipes from breakfasts to breads and crackers, main dishes and sides, and desserts. Along with a beautiful photograph of each recipe you'll find the nutritional information and a cook's note.

RESOURCES

Find additional information on health and nutrition as well as helpful information about oxalates and the low oxalate diet by visiting online websites. Some of my favorite websites for information are listed below.

Dr. Mercola
http://www.mercola.com
A great website for current health news and much more.

Loving Our Guts
http://www.lovingourguts.com
A blog website with low oxalate information and low oxalate recipes.

Low Oxalate Info
http://lowoxalateinfo.com
Helpful information about the low oxalate diet with many links to other related resources. Included in this website is information on how to get an accurate low oxalate food list.

OxVox: Talk and Tools for the Low Oxalate Diet
http://oxvox.com
You will find many articles and useful links on this very informative website. Many questions are answered in the Blog section.

The National Kidney Foundation
https://www.kidney.org/atoz/content/diet
A question and answer page about diet and kidney stones.

Printed in Great
Britain
by Amazon